A house thatched in combed wheat reed at Furze in the New Forest.

Thatch and Thatching

Jacqueline Fearn

A Shire book

Published in 2004 by Shire Publications Ltd,
Cromwell House, Church Street, Princes Risborough,
Buckinghamshire HP27 9AA, UK.
(Website: www.shirebooks.co.uk)

British Library Cataloguing in Publication Data:
Fearn, Jacqueline
Thatch and thatching. – 2nd ed. – (Shire album; 16)
1. Thatched roofs
I.Title 695
ISBN 0 7478 0588 1.

Cover: *Detail from 'The Thatcher' by George Morland (1763–1804), engraved by William Ward.*

ACKNOWLEDGEMENTS
The first edition of this book relied greatly on help from Andrew Jewell, then Keeper, and Dr Sadie B. Ward of the Museum of English Rural Life, Reading, and members of staff at the Council for Small Industries in Rural Areas, now the Countryside Agency.
For this edition the author is grateful to Dr James Moir for invaluable assistance and guidance. Help and information were also given by Peter Evans of the Countryside Agency and Gerallt Nash of the Museum of Welsh Life, St Fagans, Cardiff.
Photographs are acknowledged as follows: the Council for Small Industries in Rural Areas, now the Countryside Agency, pages 5 (top), 16 (bottom), 23, 25 (all), 26 (bottom), 27 (all), 28 (top), 29 (both), 31 (top two and bottom), 32 (both), 33 (top two and bottom), 35 (both), 36, 37 (all), 38 (top right); Cadbury Lamb, pages 1, 5 (bottom), 6 (all), 8 (top), 9 (both), 10 (top), 13 (top), 15 (bottom), 17 (top two), 18 (bottom), 24 (top), 30 (all), 31 (centre), 33 (centre), 34 (all), 38 (top left), 39 (both), 40 (all), 41 (both), 42 (top), 44 (all), 45 (bottom), 46 (bottom); London News Agency, page 28 (centre); Dr James Moir, pages 3, 7 (top), 11, 14 (bottom), 15 (top), 24 (bottom), 26 (top), 28 (bottom), 38 (bottom), 42 (bottom), 43 (both), 45 (top), 46 (top); the Museum of English Rural Life, University of Reading, pages 4, 7 (bottom), 16 (top), 17 (bottom), 18 (top three), 19 (all), 20 (all), 21; Diana Zeuner, pages 8 (bottom), 10 (bottom), 12, 13 (bottom), 14 (top), 24 (lower). The drawing on page 22 is by Ron Shaddock.

Printed in Malta by Gutenberg Press Limited, Gudja Road,
Tarxien PLA 19, Malta.

Contents

Introduction. 4

Thatching materials 12

The thatcher's tools 19

The methods of thatching 22

Choosing and living with thatch 39

Further reading. 47

Places to visit 47

Index. 48

Elegant water reed near Hunston, Bury St Edmunds, Suffolk.

Introduction

Most of us would agree that the presence of a thatched cottage in a view of the countryside adds a satisfying final touch. With its association with the unhurried past, it completes the rural scene as we think it should be. Occasionally there is the added pleasure of seeing a thatcher at work on a roof which is being splendidly renewed in bright straw or reed the colour of tarnished gold. Most people so rarely see a thatcher that it may not be appreciated that thatching is a thriving craft – there were between nine hundred and one thousand at work in 2003. While anyone can call himself a 'master thatcher' without belonging to any recognised trade body, there are two main membership societies, the National Council of Master Thatchers' Associations, formed from twelve county associations, and the National Society of Master Thatchers. These bodies can help owners to find competent thatchers, although inspection of previous work or recommendation from a knowledgeable, satisfied customer is also important.

Although most thatchers would say that the craft is learned in time on the roof, training, leading to National Vocational Qualifications, is available at Knuston Hall, Northamptonshire, to anyone who has worked as a thatcher for at least six months. This was funded and administered by the Countryside Agency in cooperation with thatchers from the two associations, but administration has now passed to the Herefordshire College of Technology.

Without prejudice to the great number of good thatchers, it is important that there should be some regulation, for very little is generally known about thatch, thatching and thatchers. There are no

Immaculate combed wheat reed at Roxton, Bedfordshire.

A wooden shed trimly thatched in heather.

British Standards for the materials used. Although model specifications are available from the membership societies, they are not always employed. Architects, surveyors, builders and building inspectors rarely possess an intimate knowledge of thatch. Local authorities charged with allocating grants and advising on policy sometimes lack the necessary expertise.

This means that the thatch owner's best protection is to inform himself and be able to judge the quality of the advice he is offered, make a well-researched choice of thatcher, be familiar with the specifications and look for the usual guarantees for building work and so on.

Any kind of roofing material was called *thaec* by the Saxons, and the act of applying it was *theccan*. As the commonest materials were vegetable, such as wheat or rye straw, reed, heather, marram grass,

Duncrun Cottier's House, now at the Ulster-American Folk Park, Omagh, Northern Ireland, came from the Magilligan area of County London-derry and was occupied until the 1950s. The thatch of marram grass is secured by ropes.

At Harry Kelly's Cottage, Cregneash Folk Park, Isle of Man, straw thatch is laid over a base of 'scraa' (turf strips) laid earth side down into the room and overlapping at the ridge. Thatch and turf are secured by ropes tied to narrow stones built into the tops of the cottage walls.

bracken and turf, 'thatch' came eventually to signify such roofing. In areas such as East Anglia waterways and marshes provided a quantity of water reed, but straw thatch was the most widespread form of roofing in Britain. Threshed straw, or *long straw*, predominated but the *combed wheat reed* tradition of the West Country, in which the stem of the straw was preserved by careful threshing only towards the top, dates at least from medieval times.

It was not unknown for large and important buildings to be thatched, such as Pevensey Castle in the fourteenth century and many churches, particularly in East Anglia. But thatch was particularly suitable for smaller buildings, not only because it was

Avebury tithe barn, Wiltshire, thatched in long straw.

Palmer's Brewery, Bridport, Dorset, thatched in Dorset reed.

Urban thatch in Bishopsgate, Norwich.

readily available and inexpensive but also because cheap walls and rafters could more easily support the light thatching material, and because extras like guttering and drainpipes were unnecessary. The major drawback, however, was the risk of fire, particularly in towns. In London it was compulsory by 1212 to give thatch a coat of whitewash to protect it from sparks, and new houses thereafter were not allowed to be thatched. Other towns followed suit in due course, sometimes prompted by a serious fire, as at Wareham in Dorset, where thatch was prohibited only after the fire of 1762. But some urban examples can still be seen in cities such as Norwich.

From the late eighteenth century thatching began to decline, affected by the practical and scientific advances of the Agricultural and Industrial Revolutions. Readily available slate and tiles carried by the canals and railways, selective cereal breeding, the introduction of the threshing machine (which bruised the wheat stalks) and finally the combine harvester (which mashed them up) all contributed to a dramatic loss of thatched roofs, particularly in the north and south of England.

Thatched ricks from a bygone age.

A thatched cottage
at Codford St Mary,
Wiltshire.

Thatching increasingly became a country craft but even so came close to collapse after the Second World War when good thatching straw and skilled craftsmen were in short supply and labour costs were high. From about a million in 1800, the number of thatched houses had declined to a few thousand in the 1960s. In order to halt the decline, thatchers were encouraged to use water reed, more and more of it imported, as well as combed wheat reed from specialist producers.

Until the Second World War the straw thatcher would usually have been a part-timer, employed on other jobs until his thatching skills were required. His work was not confined to buildings: until the middle of the twentieth century the thatcher was in demand in arable areas to thatch ricks. These were also part of the great traditional thanksgiving for the harvest, sometimes proudly ornamented with straw cocks, orbs and other insignia or with corn dollies. Mechanisation and polythene have today eliminated the thatcher from the farmyard, but happily not from the roof top.

Bringing in the harvest of thatching straw at the Weald & Downland Open Air Museum, West Sussex.

A thatcher forming the ridge on a house thatched in combed wheat reed at Wherwell, Hampshire.

This may seem strange at first, as it is well known that a thatched roof is expensive and a small cottage can cost a great deal to re-roof. This might not have been possible had the ownership of many picturesque cottages not passed from the indigenous inhabitants, who could not perhaps afford the now expensive luxury of thatch, to more affluent immigrants. It is pleasant and comfortable to live in an old thatched house; also people generally have become more conscious of the need to conserve traditional buildings and crafts. In this they are encouraged by bodies such as English Heritage, which has carried out a great deal of research into historic thatching methods and produced guidance (see 'Further reading') for individuals and for local authorities – many of which require owners to retain existing types of roofing material. Anyone about to rethatch or repair a thatched roof should contact the local authority conservation officer for advice on what the local policy is and what consents are required. The officer will also know what discretionary grants may be available.

So a thatcher can usually find enough to do locally and can work further afield should he need to (some thatchers advertise on the internet). In rare cases thatching runs in the family, but today it has attracted a new generation less rooted in tradition. Thatchers are usually individualists, independent of spirit and physically tough; working on a ladder in all weathers – even snow and heavy rain may not deter a thatcher – requires stamina, and it is a solitary, uncomfortable position to maintain, standing with the body twisted, dealing with apparently intractable materials, and skilfully gauging by hand and eye alone. A

A knotted ridge and duck ornaments of combed wheat reed at Othery, Somerset.

Beautifully decorated roofs on estate cottages at Old Warden, Bedfordshire.

long-straw thatcher may have an assistant working on the ground preparing the thatch but it is unusual to find two master thatchers on one roof, unless the job is very large or they are, say, father and son.

Methods of application, depending on the type of thatch, are surprisingly uniform all over Britain but the finished roofs can vary considerably. Much depends on skill, though probably more on regional tradition, but in areas where one or two thatching families have been at work for generations there may be detected distinctive trademarks, noticeable mainly in the treatment of ridges. However, the modern introduction of rooftop pheasants and other adornments has tended to dilute individual distinctiveness.

The main objective is unchanged, however. The skilled thatcher covers the roof with thatch of even depth, at appropriate pitch, and fixes it at consistent and moderate pressure to ensure that no area is more vulnerable to decay than another.

Smoke-blackened thatch

Thatch has always needed to be renewed periodically and it might be expected that straw thatch in place today is not much older than the previous rethatching. However, there is a traditional technique of 'spar coating', that is of stripping off only the top, weathered coat of straw and fixing new layers on top of the dry,

Layers of thatch.

Smoke-blackened thatch at Warwick Farm, Long Crendon, Buckinghamshire.

unweathered coats beneath. This means that there can be a thick build-up of material and that the base coats can be considerably older than the top coat. Just how old was confirmed in the late 1990s when researchers became increasingly aware that smoke-blackened timbers and thatch could be found in the roofs of very old houses. This showed that the house was once an 'open hall' with no chimney; smoke from the central fire would have escaped through the thatch itself or through louvres in the roof and through the windows. Analysis of a particular sample of thatch showed that it had survived undisturbed for five hundred years. It had survived primarily because it had been protected by successive layers of new straw but partly because the soot deposits had discouraged both insects and fungal growth. Even when chimneys were inserted much later they were pushed through the thatch leaving the lower layers undisturbed. At least two hundred historic examples have been found and there are probably more, mainly in the south of England, particularly Devon.

While it is extraordinary that there should be such survivals, there is added archaeological value in the preservation of cereal and other crop remains, because various other types of vegetable material were mixed in with the straw. These base coats contain the best-preserved late-medieval cereal remains ever recovered in western Europe.

Thatchers may strip an old roof completely so that they can fix new thatch securely or repair old rafters or battens. This may not always be necessary and should be investigated first. The English Heritage Guidance Note *Thatch and Thatching* (see 'Further reading') explains what to do. Unless there are exceptional circumstances, layers of historic thatch should always be preserved *in situ*.

Cutting wheat grown for thatching straw with a tractor-drawn reaper-binder at the Weald & Downland Open Air Museum, West Sussex. The crop is Maris Widgeon.

Thatching materials

Straw

For centuries the commonest thatching material everywhere was the straw left after harvesting corn. Rye was the favourite for thatching but wheat straw was the most generally used, oat and barley straw being used only as a last resort. Wheat for thatching is best harvested when slightly green so that it is not brittle and yields a little in handling, and a winter-grown crop is the best. The straw generally used to be stooked, ricked, then sold by weight. Unfortunately, good thatching straw – both for long straw and combed wheat reed – became progressively harder to come by in the twentieth century because the combine harvester breaks up the straw, making it unsuitable for thatching. So thatching straw must still be specially cut with the old-fashioned binder.

Even if the harvest can be brought in without breaking up the stalks, modern high-yield wheat crops are too short in the stem and too pithy in the centre to please the thatcher (medieval reed straw could grow to more than 5 feet (1.5 metres). However, a cross between wheat and rye, *Triticale*, which tolerates poorer soils, has been introduced. Some thatchers claim that it is more durable than wheat whereas others view it with suspicion because of its hybrid origin. Materials such as South African veldt grass have been imported but, aside from how appropriate they look in Britain, it has not yet been discovered how long they last in the British climate.

Stooks of straw for roofs at the Weald & Downland Open Air Museum.

Some farmers used to set aside a few acres for growing the long-stemmed varieties. Thatchers might arrange to harvest these themselves, endeavouring to keep down costs by returning the grain to the farmer after careful threshing. This was not usual as the thatcher was too busy and liked to buy his straw. Most often he would inspect the stems, either in the field before harvest or in the rick, and test that they were hollow, checking for length – between 2 feet 6 inches and 4 feet (76 and 122 cm), and for suppleness, coarseness and straightness. It became apparent to some small farmers that growing straw for thatching could be profitable and from the 1950s and 1960s specialist producers began supplying straw, particularly combed wheat reed. Today old reaper-binders, threshers, combers, trussers and even some innovative new machines are being used in the profitable industry of growing thatching straw.

Older strains of wheat such as Maris Huntsman and Maris Widgeon are most suitable for thatching. Research into other varieties is underway, but growing, cultivating and distributing them is restricted by overbearing legislation. In addition, problems with the quality of the straw in the 1970s and 1980s highlighted the significance of there being too much nitrate in the crop as this can encourage microbacterial growth and the consequent degrading of the fitted thatch. The best straw comes from winter wheat on moderate to heavy soils with little use of artificial fertiliser and agrochemicals (to minimise the nitrate levels) but occasional use of herbicide

Sheaves of thatching straw stooked to dry in Somerset. Note how green it has been cut.

Thatched roofs on the National Trust Holnicote Estate, Somerset.

where necessary. It is reaped before it is fully ripe, then bound and stooked for about two weeks, allowing the heads to ripen without taking strength from the straw. After further ripening in a corn stack the wheat is threshed according to its future use as combed wheat reed or long straw.

Although some straw used now comes from eastern Europe, there is increasing interest in and research into greater production in Britain. At the Holnicote Estate in Somerset the National Trust is running a project to grow older varieties and to study how the straw performs on estate buildings.

Long straw

Long-straw thatching was once the commonest form in most parts of England. It has been said that some cottages look more thatched than others, indicating a noticeable difference and, perhaps, a more rustic finish. This arises from its preparation on the ground. The threshed straw is shaken into a layered bed (heads and butts mixed), wetted and then drawn in handfuls from the bed and formed into tight, compact,

Long straw with a flush ridge at Duston, Northamptonshire.

Long straw at Odell, Bedfordshire.

tapering *yealms* about 18 by 24 by 5 inches deep (46 by 61 by 13 cm) – the dimensions vary. Because the straw is jumbled it cannot be dressed into place and this, together with a tendency to swell above its fixings, gives it a more rounded, poured-on, pie-crust appearance than other thatches. The eaves and gables are always finished with long rods or *liggers* to help control the looser mixed ends of the straw. On close inspection both butt ends and ears of wheat are visible on the surface and the ends are trimmed at the gables.

Although block-cut ridges, where the surface of the ridge rises above the surface of the main coat, have appeared in recent years, the ridge on long-straw roofs is traditionally finished flush with the roof slope and secured by decorative liggers.

Combed wheat reed

Archaeological evidence has confirmed that the combed wheat reed tradition of the West Country dates back at least to about 1400. The straw was carefully grown for thatching, reaped into sheaves, threshed towards the top of the stem and combed to remove weeds and short

Thatcher Trevor Lewis tying straw into nitches for application as combed wheat reed. Note the length of straw required for thatching.

Left: *Feeding wheat on to the top tier of the reed-comber. Note the grain piling up on the left.*

straw, thus producing the clean, aligned stems, butt ends all pointing the same way, known as combed wheat reed. These were then laid in the same way as water reed, with only the ends of the straw exposed.

With the advent of the reaper-binder in the 1860s farmers were able to harvest the wheat much faster, but at the expense of damaging the stems in the threshing drum. In the West Country an iron-toothed comb within a combing box was devised to bypass the drum. Today the wheat for thatching is still cut by binder and then passed through to the comber to strip the heads (which go through to the thresher) and comb the straw, which, butt ends aligned, is conveyed on belts to a trusser and tied into bundles, each weighing about 28 pounds (12.7 kg). These are butted to level the ends and then trimmed. Modern heavy-headed wheats are as unsuitable for combed wheat reed thatching as they are for long straw.

A roof of combed wheat reed can look as smooth and manicured as one of water reed and it is often difficult to detect the difference. The ridge is traditionally flush, but it may be block-cut and characteristically peaked at the gable ends.

Water reed

The only other principal alternative to thatching straw is water reed (*Phragmites communis*). It grows in water, the best in salt water, and is commonest in marshy estuaries. In Britain it is found principally in Norfolk, the Fenland and a little in Dorset (Abbotsbury Spear). It grows from 4 to 8 feet (1.2 to 2.4 metres) tall and cannot be harvested until the frost has killed the long leaves or 'flag' on the main stem. In practice the reed is rarely cut before December and harvesting continues through the winter months until the young shoots begin to appear in March and April. Regular cutting is the only method of cultivation, as the straight, sturdy structure of the reed is impaired when it has stood in ever thickening bunches for a number of years. After cutting, the reed is tied into bundles 12 inches (30 cm) in diameter and stacked in 'fathoms' or groups of six. Wading through the icy water to cut reed with a scythe or sickle was an uninviting and slow job, and areas of potentially useful reed sometimes remained uncut. Following

Bundles of straw showing the stems, butt ends together, reed style, for combed wheat reed thatching.

Right: *Loading some of the 7500 bundles of water reed cut at Cley Marshes in Norfolk during the winter of 2003/4.*

Below: *A boat stacked with Norfolk reed.*

mechanisation on the farm, machines were adapted to cut reed, greatly increasing productivity, but for some time Norfolk has not been able to supply sufficient reed and since the 1970s imports of water reed from eastern Europe have expanded rapidly.

Unlike long straw, water reed is laid so that only the butt ends of the stalk are exposed, bristling outwards so that water is shed from tip to tip on its way down the roof. The reed is secured very tightly under tension – otherwise fine stems would slip out – and spars and liggers secure the traditional block-cut ridge, usually formed from sedge, a tough marsh plant. Water reed cannot be bent over to form a ridge as straw can and straw ridges were once common but latterly sedge has been used instead.

Sedge and heather

Other materials occasionally used for thatching are sedge and heather. Sedge is used to ridge both straw and reed roofs in Norfolk and was used in times of reed shortages to coat whole roofs – a nasty job with a very rough material. Like water reed, sedge is a marsh plant, but with a rougher, rush-like leaf. Ideally it is cut when green, although it can be cut all the year round.

Heather was once in general use in upland areas where corn was not grown, such as the north-east of England and Scotland. It was cut in autumn while still in bloom and laid with the roots intertwined and pointing upwards. Heather thatch can still be seen in Northumbria. Its least attractive feature, perhaps, is the heavy black colour the heather turns to as it dries.

Rethatching a roof of heather.

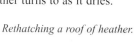

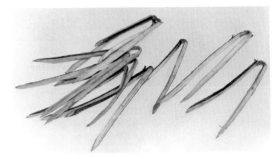

Above: *Hazel spars.*

Left: *Splitting a hazel spar-gadd (length of unsplit hazel) with a spar hook.*

A spar hook.

Spars, liggers and sways

Roundwood sections of coppiced hazel (and sometimes willow) are used for making *spars* (or broaches), *liggers* (or rods) and *sways*. Spars are short, half-inch (13 mm) wide lengths that are twisted to make staples for packing the straw tightly together and securing at certain stages; very long, half-inch-wide lengths are used for the external liggers or runners that secure the ridge and, in long straw, the eaves and barges (gables); long, 1 inch (25 mm) wide rods called sways hold down each new course of thatch, although increasingly metal rods, wires and fixings are used.

Thatcher Trevor Lewis on the roof twisting a spar.

Some thatchers still coppice their own hazel and coppicing has been revived in parts of southern England, largely for garden products, and spars and sways are available from specialist coppice workers.

Temporary sways, to be removed as the work is permanently secured, are made from twisted straw or small handfuls of reed.

The thatcher's tools

Thatching tools vary according to the thatcher, the material in use and the locality. There are many alternative regional names for any tool mentioned here. It is possible to apply thatch without any special tools at all or with improvised ones; the craft lies in the skill of the thatcher. However, most thatchers will probably have certain basic items, such as ladders, although scaffolding has replaced them in some areas.

All thatch is sharp or prickly so the thatcher will often wear some protection, usually of leather, on his leaning arm, on his beating hand and on his knees. Long straw is most often carried in a V-shaped yoke, which

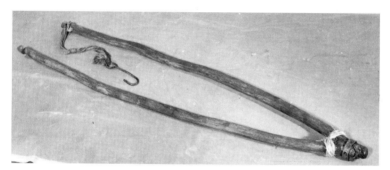

Above: *An old long-straw yoke.*

Right: *Thatching needles.*

Traditional knee pads.

Dressing thatch with a leggatt on a ridge of water reed over a slate roof.

Right: *A leggatt for combed wheat reed, showing the ridges.*

Thatching shears.

A side-rake in use on long straw.

is secured by a leather thong or cord. Often some sort of cradle or 'horse', which can be fixed to the roof, is used to hold the material about to be used. Iron hooks and needles, from 6 to 12 inches (15 to 30 cm) long, are used to hold material in position and as levers to push the stalks close together.

There are all sorts of knives and shearing hooks for cleaning down and trimming, but a long-straw thatcher will have a long-handled and long-bladed knife to trim the eaves. Reed thatch is dressed with a bat or leggatt ('biddle' in the West Country). This consists of a handle attached to a rectangle of wood about 10 by 8 inches (25 by 20 cm) which is either ridged (for wheat reed) or nailed (for water reed) on the underside. A long-straw thatcher will have a side-rake to comb out the waste. All thatchers have shears and reed thatchers have spot boards on which to bang the bunches to level the ends.

The methods of thatching

The methods of applying all three materials are similar but require some different skills; most thatchers will offer any of the three types.

When a roof is to be thatched account has to be taken of one or two special factors, starting with its pitch. This is a very complicated area, as there are so many elements affecting the pitch of the finished roof apart from the pitch of the rafters. The finished pitch of an existing roof is influenced, of course, by the pitch it starts with, but it may be affected, for example, by the thickness of base coats left in place and by the angle at which the thatch bundles were laid. For a new roof a pitch of 50 degrees is usually recommended, although other considerations, such as the complexity of existing roof features, may dictate a slacker pitch.

The rafters must overhang the walls and a board called a *tilting fillet* should be fitted at right angles to the rafters at the eaves end in order to force the bottom layer of thatch slightly out and up. Battens are fixed

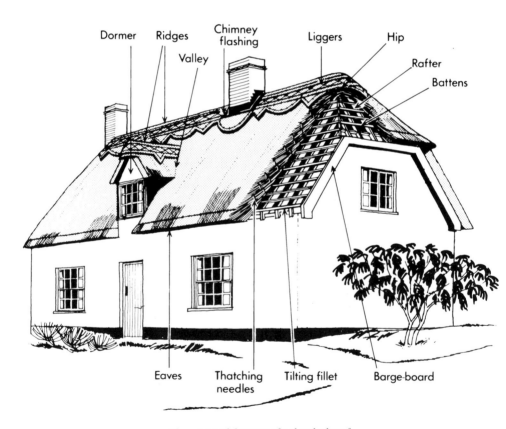

The principal features of a thatched roof.

*Rafters with
battens in place
ready for
thatching. Note
the tilting effect of
the tilting fillet on
the reed
positioned at the
far end.*

horizontally across the rafters. At the gables a barge-board is sometimes fixed on the last rafter. Windows have to be similarly treated and the areas round both the windows and the chimneys have to be prepared so that the thatch will flow evenly, enabling lead or mortar seals to be inserted while the thatch retains an even pitch and the water flow is unimpeded.

Because water reed has to be fixed under greater tension, rethatching usually involves stripping back to the rafters. For long straw and combed wheat reed the thatcher strips off only as much as is necessary (bearing in mind that the battens may need repairing), leaving a layer as a lining for the new work. The practice of 'spar coating' – thatching over previous work – is traditional and means that much earlier layers of historic thatch may be preserved below the surface layer and should not be removed (see page 10).

The thatcher needs to know before he starts work how much long straw, wheat reed or water reed he will need, and the customer will almost certainly want an estimated cost. Generally the roof area is measured and the price assessed in terms of cost per 'square', which is 100 square feet (9.3 square metres), quantities of material required, and other factors such as necessary repairs, complexity of roof features and consequent timescale. Such unit costing is businesslike and reassuring for the customer but not all thatchers like it and some prefer to give an overall price. It is up to the customer to use his judgement, based on some understanding of the materials about to be used and how they are to be applied, what guarantees are offered and what is excluded.

Long straw at Wistanstow, Shropshire.

Chris Tomkins rethatching Hangleton Cottage at the Weald & Downland Open Air Museum, West Sussex.

Thatching in long straw

Of the three types of thatching material, long straw needs most preparation before it can be laid. It is usually spread out in layers, with mixed butts and ears, which are thoroughly wetted and then left to soak for an hour or two to make the straw pliable. Then, working in a straight line, handfuls of straw are drawn out evenly, tidied so that the straws are in line and gathered into bunches that are thicker at the bottom than at the top. These are *yealms* and as they are assembled they are laid, large end forward, in a shaped yoke that holds up to eight yealms. Special, wide yealms called *bottles* are made for the eaves; these have a splayed large end and are folded double and tied at the bent end.

Work begins at the eaves and the roof is completed in sections, some thatchers staggering the courses across the roof, others working upwards in lanes about 30 inches (76 cm) wide. The first bottles are laid at 45 degrees and overhang by half the length. The bottle may be tied in with tarred cord or swayed down by a sway held by hooks driven into the rafter as low as possible or sometimes into the wall plate. Each bottle is pushed hard towards the previous one by spars driven horizontally (at a slight angle to prevent water penetration) through the straw. The barge (gable) is treated similarly, the barge sway and first

Left: *Driving a spar horizontally through one long-straw bottle into the next to pack the straw tightly.*

Below left: *Securing the thatch with a permanent sway held in place by a long hook to retain an optimum of 9 inches (23 cm) of thatch.*

Below right: *Courses of long straw staggered across the roof showing the positions of the sways.*

Side-raking a section of work in long straw. Note that the roof has been stripped in order to replace the battens.

Long straw at Eardisland, Herefordshire.

bottle being wedged under the eaves sway for a tight join. On this bristling fringe the roof courses are built up.

Where the battens are exposed, a thin layer of straw is laid over as a tidy lining, and then the first roof course is started at the same angle as and very low on the bottle and is sparred down just below the eaves sway with a twisted straw bond. This makes a double course to give the desired eaves thickness of up to 18 inches (45 cm). Succeeding courses are laid overlapping the previous one by two-thirds and are permanently swayed down after every two courses. The straw is tightly pushed between needles and each section is tidied and often side-raked.

Chimneys and windows need careful treatment to maintain the smooth lines and the rain-shedding angles of the laid straw. The lead flashings above a free-standing chimney lead up under the thatch, which is cut off several inches from the chimney, forming a gully into which the water flows. The flashing extends over the thatch at the sides so the water runs on to the thatch. Alternatively, the lead or mortar is laid over the thatch and up round the chimney like a collar. Valleys, where two roofs meet, are packed with straw to form a smooth curve.

When the ridge is reached, a roll of straw is tied on to the ridge-board and more bottles are swayed down around the apex. The last yealms are sparred into each side, the small ends that meet above the ridge being sparred into the roll. For the ridge course, yealms are drawn out and equalised at top and bottom, bent across the apex and the skirts

Fixing the barge ligger. Where two lengths of hazel join, their ends are held together under a spar.

Laying a good foundation for the ridge course. The ridge roll (top right) is in position.

Pushing the straw of bent yealms together with a needle to make a tight ridge.

Above: *Lead flashing fitted like a collar round the chimney and over the ridge.*

Below: *Trimming the gable with a long-handled knife, allowing an overhang of about 4 inches (10 cm).*

Trimming the eaves of long-straw thatch.

An old and unusual picture of long-straw thatching in progress. Note the splendid ladder.

Long-straw thatch thirty-five years old at Orchard-side, Box End, Bedford-shire.

A skilfully decorated long-straw ridge near Eye, Suffolk, with unusual rolled barges.

forced tightly down. The top ligger is laid along the ridge and sparred down. Liggers are secured on either side and decorative spar patterns sparred down before the skirts are cut to shape. The barge liggers meet and form a point, underneath which it may be necessary to pack more straw before finally fixing. The barges are then cut with the long-handled knife and trimmed with shears. Finally, the main body of the roof and the eaves are raked and neatly trimmed.

Thatching in combed wheat reed

Combed wheat reed usually comes to the thatcher in the bundles or *nitches* he will use, each weighing 28 pounds (12.7 kg). The nitches are tidied, butted on the spot board to even the ends, sprinkled with water through the top end and turned on one side to soak for a while.

The eaves and barges are laid with *wadds*, extra large handfuls of reed butted and then tied firmly together. A staple and cord are fixed in the corner and a hazel sway is nailed close to the barge-board to provide a fixing for the barge wadds. The corner wadd is tied in at an angle by

Rethatching cottages in combed wheat reed in Wendover, Buckinghamshire. Work on the roof on the right has been completed.

Combed wheat reed tied into nitches.

Right: *The second cottage roof at Wendover stripped to a firm coat for rethatching.*

lacing round the wadd, over the sway and then the batten, and pulling tight. The succeeding wadds are laced to the batten, the barge wadds to the sway. To align and tighten the wadds in the cord the butts are dressed with the leggatt as the work proceeds.

Where battens are exposed, the courses are laid on a back-filling of straw. Half a nitch of reed is butted on the roof to establish the pitch, laid in the corner and held in position with one arm while the butts are dressed into position. The reed is secured with a temporary sway and the butts are dressed with the leggatt. When sufficient reed is in place it is properly swayed down with a sway secured by an iron nail or by a spar if into an existing coat, or by stitching. Each bunch is tightly packed next to another and held in place temporarily by an iron needle. The temporary sway is released as required.

Butting the nitch on the roof to align and bevel the butts.

Dressing the eaves wadds to tighten them in the cord.

Cutting the twine around the next wadd, held in the cradle.

Fixing a permanent sway. The rafter has been located with the needle and the hook is being positioned. Note the temporary straw sway below.

Trimming the combed wheat reed with a shearing hook.

Chimneys and dormers are treated in the same way as with long straw.

The ridge is based on a tightly packed roll of reed about 4 inches (10 cm) thick and varying in length according to the ridge length. The tops of the course that oversail the ridge are twisted and folded back, the twisted knuckles being forced against each other and secured by a reed sway sparred into the ridge roll. At the apex wadds are laid thickly over the top and sparred into the roll. A second, smaller roll is sparred through into the first. The next pattern course is laid with large handfuls of reed, their small ends folded under and placed so that they end just above the top of the roll, just meeting those laid on the other side of the roof. A third, small roll is now sparred down and a ligger is started to run across the ridge. The ridge course is laid by taking an evened-out

Twisting the oversailing ends of combed wheat reed at the ridge.

Above: *Sparring down the third ridge ligger.*

Right: *Cross-section through the combed wheat reed showing the construction of the courses and the ridge rolls.*

bunch of reed, bending it in half and positioning it under the ligger. A vertical needle levers the reeds together. Side liggers are sparred into position. Cross liggers are decoratively placed and the required pattern is cut at the ends. On a good ridge the top will be very narrow and the depth of thatch some 18 inches (45 cm). In some parts of the West Country thatchers finish with extended or upturned pinnacles at the gable ends: on the porch illustrated below, a characteristic 'coxcomb' bristles above the ridge. Finally there will be a last beating up with the leggatt and a light trim with the shearing hook.

A porch in combed wheat reed with rakishly fringed coxcomb.

Graceful roofs at Holford, Somerset.

Right: *The head gardener's cottage at Somerleyton Hall, Suffolk, thatched in water reed and ridged with sedge.*

Thatching in water reed

The bunches of reed as delivered to the site will probably still need to be graded into long, short and coarse categories, long reed being needed for the eaves, short for the barges, and coarse for general work. Bundles 12 inches (30 cm) in diameter are assembled, banged or 'butted' on the spot board to level the ends, and tied. Four to eight bundles will be taken to the roof at a time.

Work begins at the eaves and usually proceeds from right to left. A staple is fixed in the corner to secure the binding twine for the first course, and the first bundles are butted to set a bevel for the overhang. Starting at an angle, with an overhang of 2 or 3 feet (60 or 90 cm), bundles are fixed, butt ends down, the cord passing once round the bundle and twice round the batten before being double-tied. Each one is butted upwards with the leggatt to tighten the reed in the bond and

An immaculate new roof in water reed at Fakenham Magna, Norfolk, by Roger Yates of Rougham.

Above: *Butting water reed to put a bevel on the reed for the eaves course.*

An eaves course in water reed. The 45 degree angle has straightened to vertical.

The gable of water reed taking shape – part of a full course – held down by a temporary sway.

forced tightly up to the next with the needles. At a gable the barge bunches are secured under a sway parallel to the barge and close to it to hold the reed under tension. There is an overhang of some 6 inches (15 cm). Handfuls of reed are forced under the small ends lying against the rafters to provide both a lever to hold the reed under tension and a tidy back-filling.

The next course is laid well down over the first and swayed low down, temporarily with a reed bond and finally with a hazel or steel sway and iron hooks. The thatcher locates the rafter into which the hook is driven by probing with a needle. Succeeding courses are laid similarly, each completely covering the sway securing the lower course, the reed being continually dressed with the leggatt to keep the butt ends in smooth alignment all the way up the roof.

Chimneys and dormers are treated in the same way as with long straw.

As the courses approach the ridge-board, the tops of the reed project above it. Water reed will not bend over the top of the ridge, so the ends are cut off at the same angle as the approaching rafters, level with the ridge, which is then prepared for the sedge ridging. The gables are trimmed and dressed with the leggatt, then a long roll of reed, the length of the ridge and from 4 inches (10 cm) in diameter, is assembled on the ground and then fixed to the ridge. At the apex of the barge, reed is laid horizontally and swayed down over the ridge. A thick layer of damp or green sedge is assembled over the ridge, in line with the ridge courses, to form a skirt, pushed tightly together and fastened down with spars driven into the reed. A narrower roll is sparred on top of the skirt into the first roll, and over this even yealms of sedge are bent to form a

Reed laid horizontally at the apex to form a firm base for the sedge ridge.

Laying the final ridge course with sedge yealms drawn out over the top.

Above: *Sparring down the beginning of the top ligger on a sedge ridge. The sedge will be pushed tightly under this ligger.*

Behind a chimney, this lead gutter is fitted under the thatch, which will shed water into it for dispersal over the thatch below.

Above: *A gable in water reed with a pattern cut into the body of the thatch as well as the ridge, at Abbots Ripton, Cambridgeshire.*

Left: *At Martham, Norfolk, twenty-year-old thatch is being re-capped with sedge.*

wrapover top. This is sparred firmly down with liggers about 12 inches (30 cm) apart and a vertical barge ligger. Any decorative diagonal liggers are sparred down and the edges of the skirt are block-cut into decorative shapes. The final tidying operation follows with the clipping of odd ends and the removal of loose bits.

Norfolk reed at Biddenham, Bedfordshire.

The thatched windmill at High Ham, Somerset.

Choosing and living with thatch

It is still picturesque and unusual to see a thatcher on a roof but, far from being a bucolic laid-back rural activity, thatching is thriving. Thatchers are highly mobile businessmen like any others in the building industry. Their trade is supported by companies vying to provide reasonably priced insurance cover for the property, particularly if a variety of fire-retardant measures have been included in the work. In some places new houses with thatched roofs are being built.

   Thatched houses are undoubtedly important landscape features and until the second half of the twentieth century would usually have been thatched in local styles with locally grown materials. However, during that period attention turned to the length of time a roof in any of the

Abernodwydd Farmhouse, built in 1678 at Llangadfan, Powys, re-erected at the Museum of Welsh Life, St Fagans, near Cardiff, in 1955 and thatched in combed wheat reed.

materials might last. Statistics were published in the 1960s based on figures for straw fixed in the 1940s and 1950s; these reflected the poor quality of the straw then available. Such straw is not comparable to the much better straw produced by specialist growers today. Not taken into account were issues specific to the individual case such as the situation of the building, the local climate, the pitch of the roof, the fitness of the material for the roof shape, the quality of the material used, the skill of the thatcher, the standard of the finished work and the subsequent

Nant Wallter Cottage, built at Taliaris, Carmarthenshire, about 1770, re-erected at the Museum of Welsh Life in 1993. The roof of this clay-walled cottage is formed of crucks on which wattle, gorse and finally straw thatch were laid.

Right: *Built in the late eighteenth century, Leagrave Cottage originally stood in Leagrave, near Luton, Bedfordshire. It was re-erected and thatched in long straw at the Chiltern Open Air Museum, Chalfont St Giles, Buckinghamshire.*

A straw-thatched stack of sheep hurdles on the village green at Priddy in Somerset. The village has held an annual sheep fair for over six hundred years and local legend holds that the fair will cease if these old hurdles are removed.

Water-reed thatch on the Affleck Arms, Dalham, Suffolk.

maintenance of the roof, all factors that later research has shown to be fundamental. Long straw lost the statistical battle and, as good long straw was hard to find and planning consent was not required for a change of thatching material, as it would have been, for example, for slate to replace tile, so thatchers were at liberty to fix whatever material the owner preferred: it did not seem to be a question to concern anyone else.

Attitudes have changed, however: environmental awareness as well as aesthetic considerations have highlighted the value of our traditional landscapes, their distinctive features and regional styles. Research and the development of satisfactory thatching straw have also encouraged conservation bodies, including English Heritage, and local authorities to advocate like-for-like replacement, and owners seeking to change the material will need to obtain planning consent if the building is listed, as

Shade and shelter under water reed at Walberswick, Suffolk.

New thatch at Dorchester-on-Thames, Oxfordshire.

nearly three-quarters of thatched buildings are. The debate goes on, however, based partly on the former scarcity of good long straw and partly on evidence gathered in the mid twentieth century.

So, although all three types of thatch have characteristics to be preserved, it is clearly local long-straw traditions that are mainly at risk. Not all houses benefit from the precise lines imposed by the reeds, particularly water reed. Roofs where reed has replaced long straw can appear too smart and box-like, small dormers dispro-portionately bulky, differing roof heights too pronounced. Lost are the gentle, slightly undulating lines of long straw that suited the form of the house and were part of the local tradition, and lost, too, may be the necessary thatching skills. Many

Below: *Long-straw thatch on Folly Cottage near Luston, Herefordshire.*

Roxton chapel, Bedford-shire, thatched in water reed.

experienced thatchers, working within their own traditions, have never fitted long straw, while others, certainly in Buckinghamshire, offer a so-called 'hybrid thatch' of combed wheat reed that is finished with the long-straw features of hazel-rod patterns at the gables and eaves.

One thatcher told the author that he would thatch round a wheelbarrow if he found it on the roof at the appropriate pitch with battens in place; he regarded thatch as a roof fit for any type of building. However, it has predominated in the areas of cob-mud and clay-lump wall construction, such as Devon and the south-west of England and it looks particularly well with limewashed and pastel walls, as in East Anglia. Timber-clad and timber-framed walls set it off and it is not out of place with stone, as in moorland areas. Where thatch did decline most sharply in popularity, such as in the industrial north, the availability of slate and clay tiles probably complemented the desire for roofing that would permanently withstand cold, wet weather conditions.

Nowadays most thatched roofs will be covered with galvanised wire or plastic netting to keep out the birds and vermin, and it can be

A picturesque cottage at Blaise Hamlet on the Blaise Castle estate near Bristol.

Above: *A row of thatched cottages at Lackford, Suffolk.*

advocated in windy situations. Some thatchers will not guarantee a roof that is not netted, although there is a view that netting should be used only when necessary to prevent sustained and significant attack. For easier removal in case of fire, wire netting should be laid vertically from ridge to eaves with edges flush; plastic netting, which is fitted as a single sheet, has to be cut free and slows down removal.

All netting can form a trap for falling leaves, which encourage damp, impede the flow of rain down the roof, and thus contribute to moss and lichen growth. As part of routine maintenance, the timing of which depends on the prevailing conditions, the leaves and twigs should be

removed and moss and lichen carefully scraped and brushed away – without the use of possibly harmful chemicals. After all, the thatcher has carefully shaped the thatch over or under chimney flashing and packed the valleys to form gentle shedding lines,

Left: *Whitewash and thatch at Glamis, Angus, Scotland.*

Thatched roofs at Southend on the Ridgeway near Ogbourne St George in Wiltshire.

A long and deep barn roof at Blewbury, Oxfordshire.

his whole craft devoted to the efficient shedding of water by a material that might be expected to absorb it. In a proper state of repair, thatch will never be wet beyond an inch or two of its thickness and the original colour of fresh straw or reed is revealed underneath when the roof is prepared for rethatching.

During the life of the thatch the ridge will need to be replaced perhaps two or three times, giving a good opportunity to strip the netting, patch vulnerable areas – especially valleys and chimney flanks – and scrape away moss and lichen. It is important routinely to assess and maintain the thatch, especially as it gets older, as it may be that patching and cleaning will postpone rethatching.

Fire is a hazard to any property but obviously dry thatch will burn more readily than other forms of roof. Insurance companies are very conscious of this and premiums are higher for thatched houses and their contents, but less so when some fire-prevention measures are incorporated. Tests by the Fire Research Station showed that a thatched roof constructed so that the thatch is separated from the roof void by a fire-resisting barrier is easier to extinguish and there is far less damage from fire-fighting water. For existing roofs the fire-resisting barrier would usually be underneath the thatch, between the rafters; new roofs would be constructed with the barrier in place on top of the rafters.

The practice of soaking the straw in fire-retardant solution before it was laid has been

A thatched summerhouse in the restored Master's Garden at the Lord Leycester Hospital, Warwick.

Rural elegance at Old Warden, Bedfordshire.

abandoned because the chemicals were shown to break down the cell structure of the straw and so shorten its life. The alternative method of spraying the finished roof with fire-tested silicon-based compounds lasts about ten years, but it is uncertain how this affects the breathing of the thatch.

Owners should also make sure that their chimneys, which should end well above the highest point of the roof, are safe and routinely maintained, not only to prevent the escape of smoke and fire but also to prevent heat conduction to the thatch. Methods are now available of lining chimneys and fitting them with special heat sensors and other warning devices. The excellent booklet *A Guide to Fire Safety in Thatched Buildings* (FSN 71, 1999), produced by the Dorset Fire and Rescue Service, covers all aspects of fire retardancy and is essential reading.

The final word on thatch must be said from the inside. There is no pleasanter roof to live under – it provides excellent insulation to keep the warmth in during the winter and out during the summer. Often thatch is associated with sloping ceilings in the bedrooms, which, with their thatch covering and protected windows, are quiet because thatch also soundproofs very well. The modern versions of this apparently archaic form of roof still provide the most comfortable protection from the weather.

A kangaroo as a thatch ornament in Godshill, Isle of Wight.

Further reading

Brockett, Peter, and Wright, Adela. *The Care and Repair of Thatched Roofs* (Technical Pamphlet 10). Society for the Protection of Ancient Buildings (37 Spital Square, London E1 6DY) and Rural Development Commission, 1986.

Cox, J., and Letts, J. *Thatch: Thatching in England 1940–1994* (English Heritage Research Transactions 6). James & James, 2000.

Cox, J., and Thorp, John R. L. *Devon Thatch: An Illustrated History of Thatching and Thatched Buildings in Devon.* Devon Books, Halsgrove Publishing, 2001.

Dorset Fire and Rescue Service. *A Guide to Fire Safety in Thatched Buildings* (FSN 71). Dorset County Council (County Hall, Dorchester DT1 1XJ), 1999.

Letts, J. *Smoke-Blackened Thatch: A New Source of Medieval Plant Remains from Southern England.* English Heritage and the University of Reading, 1999.

Moir, J., and Letts, J. *Thatch: Thatching in England 1790–1940* (English Heritage Research Transactions 5). James & James, 1999.

Nash, J. *Thatchers and Thatching.* Batsford, 1991.

Salzman, L. F. *Building in England Down to 1540.* Oxford University Press, 1952. Special edition, Sandpiper Books, 1997.

Thatch and Thatching (English Heritage Guidance Note). English Heritage, 2000.

The Thatcher's Craft. The Countryside Agency (John Dower House, Crescent Place, Cheltenham, Gloucestershire GL50 3RA), 1961; reprinted 1988.

West, R. C. *Thatch: A Manual for Owners, Surveyors, Architects and Builders.* David & Charles, 1989.

Places to visit

Visitors are advised to confirm dates and hours of opening before travelling.

Avoncroft Museum of Historic Buildings, Redditch Road, Stoke Heath, Bromsgrove, Worcestershire B60 4JR. Telephone: 01527 831363 or 831886. Website: www.avoncroft.org.uk

Bewdley Museum, The Shambles, Load Street, Bewdley, Worcestershire DY12 2AE. Telephone: 01299 403573.

Bicton Park Countryside Museum, East Budleigh, Budleigh Salterton, Devon EX9 7BJ. Telephone: 01395 568465. Website: www.bictongardens.co.uk

Breamore Countryside Museum, Breamore House, Breamore, Fordingbridge, Hampshire SP6 2BY. Telephone: 01725 512233. Website: www.hants.gov.uk

Chiltern Open Air Museum, Newland Park, Gorelands Lane, Chalfont St Giles, Buckinghamshire HP8 4AB. Telephone: 01494 871117. Website: www.coam.org.uk

Cregneash Village Folk Museum, Cregneash, Isle of Man IM9 5PT. Telephone: 01624 648000. Website: www.gov.im/mnh

Dorset County Museum, High West Street, Dorchester, Dorset DT1 1XA. Telephone: 01305 262735. Website: www. dorsetcountymuseum.org

Museum of East Anglian Life, Abbots Hall, Stowmarket, Suffolk IP14 1DL. Telephone: 01449 612229. Website: www.eastanglianlife.org.uk

Museum of English Rural Life, The University, Whiteknights, Reading, Berkshire RG6 2AG. Telephone: 0118 378 8660. Website: www. ruralhistory.org

Museum of Lakeland Life and Industry, Abbot Hall, Kendal, Cumbria LA9 5AL. Telephone: 01539 772464. Website: www.lakelandmuseum.org.uk

Museum of Lincolnshire Life, The Old Barracks, Burton Road, Lincoln LN1 3LY. Telephone: 01522 528448. Website: www.lincolnshire.gov.uk

Museum of Welsh Life, St Fagans, Cardiff CF5 6XB. Telephone: 029 2057 3500. Website: www.nmgw.ac.uk

North Cornwall Museum and Gallery, The Clease, Camelford, Cornwall PL32 9PL. Telephone: 01840 212954.

Oxfordshire County Museum, Fletcher's House, Park Street, Woodstock, Oxfordshire OX20 1SN. Telephone: 01993 811456. Website: www.oxfordshire.gov.uk

Roots of Norfolk, Gressenhall, Dereham, Norfolk NR20 4DR. Telephone: 01362 869263. Website: www.norfolk.gov.uk/tourism

Rutland County Museum, Catmose Street, Oakham, Rutland LE15 6HW. Telephone: 01572 758440. Website: www.rutnet.co.uk/rccmuseum

Ulster-American Folk Park, Castletown, Omagh, Co. Tyrone, Northern Ireland BT78 5QY. Telephone: 028 8224 3292. Website: www.folkpark.com

Weald & Downland Open Air Museum, Singleton, Chichester, West Sussex PO18 0EU. Telephone: 01243 811363. Website: www.wealddown.co.uk

Index

Page numbers in italic refer to illustrations.

Barge board *22*, 23
Bat *21*
Battens *22*, *23*, 25
Biddle *20, 21*
Bottles 24
Chimneys *22*, 26, *27*, *37*
Cradle 21, *31*
Combed wheat reed 6; bundles *16*; cross-section *33*; harvesting 15-16; method of thatching 29-33
Dormer *22*
Dressing the wadds *31*
Eaves *22*; trimming 28
English Heritage 9, 11
Estimates 23
Fire 7, 45-6; retardancy 44-6
Hazel spars 18, *18*; spar gadd *18*; spar patterns 29
Heather 5, 17, *17*
Hip *22*
Historic thatch 10-11, *11*, 23
Hybrid thatch 43
Knee pads *19*
Lead flashing 26, *27*
Leggatt *20*, 21
Liggers 18, *22*, *26, 33*
Listed Building consent 41-2
Local authority policy 9
Long-handled knife 21, *27*
Long straw 6, 14-15; yoke *19*; method of thatching 24-9
Maintenance 44-5
Marram grass 5, *5*
National Council of Master Thatchers' Associations 4
National Society of Master Thatchers 4

Netting 43-4
Nitches *14*, 29, *30*
Pattern course 32
Pinnacles 33
Pitch 22
Principles features of a thatched roof *22*
Rafters *22*, 23
Reaper-binder *12*, 13
Reed-comber *16*
Ridge 15, *22*, 26, *27*, *32*, 36, 37; replacing 45
Ridge roll 26, *27*
Sedge 17, 36, *37*
Shearing hook 21, *32*
Side-rake 21, *21*
Side-raking 25
Smoke-blackened thatch 10-11, *11*
Spar coating 23, *30*
Spar hook *18*
Spot board 21
Sways 18, *25*, *31*
Thatch ornaments *9*, *46*
Thatched ricks 7
Thatching courses 4
Thatching needles *19*, 21, *22*
Thatching shears *20*
Thatching straw 5-6, 12-14; harvesting *8, 12, 13*; cultivation 13-14; stooks *13*
Thatching tools 19-21
Tilting fillet *22*, *23*
Valley *22*, 26
Wadds 29, *31*
Water reed 8; bundles 34, *34*; butting ends level *34*; harvesting 16-17; method of thatching 34-8
Wattle, gorse and straw thatch *40*
Yealms 15, 24

Home-grown Dorset reed in Abbotsbury, Dorset.